hush about the hush music foundation

Hush is Australia's charity for bringing together music and medicine. Founded in 2000 by Melbourne's Royal Children's Hospital physician Catherine Crock, Hush has produced fourteen albums of original music to bring peace and hope to patients and their families.

Now distributed to every children's hospital in Australia, Hush albums bring together the nation's finest composers and performers to create music for tens of thousands of listeners every year. Profits from sales of Hush albums go to the children's hospitals for research and patient care.

With *The Hush Treasure Book* – a collection of short stories and illustrations by creators from all around Australia who have been inspired by the Hush vision of better patient care – Hush has expanded into an exciting new medium.

www.hush.org.au

First published in 2015 by Allen & Unwin

Copyright © in the collection, The Hush Foundation 2015
All text and illustrations copyright © their respective creators

The moral right of the contributors to be identified as the creators of this work has been asserted by them in accordance with the United Kingdom's *Copyright, Designs and Patents Act 1988*.

All rights reserved. No part of this book may be reproduced or transmitted in any form or by any means, electronic or mechanical, including photocopying, recording or by any information storage and retrieval system, without prior permission in writing from the publisher. The *Australian Copyright Act 1968* (the Act) allows a maximum of one chapter or ten per cent of this book, whichever is the greater, to be photocopied by any educational institution for its educational purposes provided that the educational institution (or body that administers it) has given a remuneration notice to the Copyright Agency (Australia) under the Act.

Allen & Unwin – Australia
83 Alexander Street, Crows Nest NSW 2065, Australia
Phone: (61 2) 8425 0100
Email: info@allenandunwin.com
Web: www.allenandunwin.com

Allen & Unwin – UK
c/o Murdoch Books, Erico House, 93–99 Upper Richmond Road, London SW15 2TG, UK
Phone: (44 20) 8785 5995
Email: info@murdochbooks.co.uk
Web: www.allenandunwin.com
Murdoch Books is a wholly owned division of Allen & Unwin Pty Ltd

A Cataloguing-in-Publication entry is available from the National Library of Australia
www.trove.nla.gov.au
A catalogue record for this book is available from the British Library

ISBN (AUS) 978 1 76011 279 0
ISBN (UK) 978 1 74336 664 6

Edited by Karen Tayleur
Cover and text design by Lee Burgemeestre
Cover and title page sculptures by Kevin Burgemeestre
Sculptures on endpapers created by Kevin Burgemeestre, Lee Burgemeestre and Ann James
Colour reproduction and photography by Splitting Image, Clayton, Victoria
This book was printed in April 2015 at Everbest Printing Co Ltd in 334 Huanshi Road South, Nansha, Guangdong, China.

the hush treasure book

hush
music foundation

ALLEN&UNWIN
SYDNEY · MELBOURNE · AUCKLAND · LONDON

a word from Cath

Dear Readers,

Welcome to *The Hush Treasure Book*. I am proud that Hush's first adventure into literature has produced the book you hold: a real treasure created by some of Australia's most highly regarded authors and illustrators.

Some of these stories are truly moving; others, just plain silly! This collection is a jumble of joy and reflection, a mixture that will whisk you away to a magical place.

For years Hush has produced albums of original music, the Hush Collection, to bring calm and joy to sick children and their families going through difficult times. My experiences as a children's doctor inspired our journey.
Many wonderful and generous people have joined us along the way.
Now we have started the Hush Library – what a milestone!

I'm extremely grateful to the hardworking Hush book-making group, the Hush volunteers and the talented artists of every medium who have lent their efforts to bringing *The Hush Treasure Book* to life. It has been a colourful, creative process full of surprises. I hope you, our readers, will find the fun just as infectious!

Warmest regards,

Cath

contents

WE CAN SEE THE WORLD FROM HERE JANE GODWIN & ANNA WALKER 4
NOTHING TO BE SCARED OF DOUG MACLEOD & CRAIG SMITH 6
THE ELEPHANT BIRD TOHBY RIDDLE 8
FLYING HOME ALISON LESTER 10
THE LONG SHADOW BOB GRAHAM 12
MY SHADOW KAREN BRIGGS & PAUL SEDEN 13
DOCTOR MADDIE DANNY KATZ & MITCH VANE 15
OLIVER'S TOWN NICK BLAND 18
GHOST MOTEL MICHAEL CAMILLERI & JACKIE FRENCH 20
THE MAZE PAGE JUDITH ROSSELL 24
WARD SHAUN TAN 26
I AM THE SMALL GREEN PEA STEPHEN MICHAEL KING & GLENDA MILLARD 28
BISCUIT AND BONES MARK GREENWOOD & FRANÉ LESSAC 30
DOT THE TOT ANN JAMES & KAREN TAYLEUR 32
THE BEST HORSE OF ALL JULIE VIVAS & MARGARET WILD 35
RECIPE TO CATCH A WISH JACQUI GRANTFORD 38
POPPY CHRIS MCKIMMIE 40
GRANDMA'S TREASURE VICTORIA ROHAN & JANE TANNER 42
FREE TO FLY BRUCE WHATLEY 44
CONTRIBUTORS 46

We can see the world from here

Let us go then, take my hand,
Let's run down the track and onto the sand,
Let's crawl through the tunnel, let's cross the sea,
We'll go together, you and me.

Under the trees with shadows long
Let's make up our own travelling song,
As the afternoon grows into the night
(Don't let that owl give you a fright!).

We'll get to the morning of a brand new day
We'll be nearly there, we'll be on our way
With the birds above and the fish below,
And bugs and the beetles and creatures that glow.

And we'll come to a place I want you to see
I hope that you like it, it's special to me,
It's quiet and cosy and soft like a hug
From someone you care for or someone you love.

And we can see the world from here
The city, the mountains, the water so clear
Under the shadows and into the sun
We can share this with everyone.

Let's sit in our place, the sun's made it warm
We can shelter here from the rain and the storm
Let's dangle our feet, let's shout out, let's cheer
Because we can see the world from here.

JANE GODWIN & ANNA WALKER

Nothing to be scared of

In the west, the sun is setting
Shadows slowly crawl.
Night approaches, gently, deeply,
Darkness covers all.

Orange streetlamps shine their hardest,
Still it's not enough.
Night, the silent visitor,
Is made of stronger stuff.

People in their tiny houses,
Lock their doors up tight.
Children peep from bedroom windows,
Frightened of the night.

DOUG MACLEOD & CRAIG SMITH

When at last the town is sleeping,
Moving shapes appear.
Streetlights catch them for a moment,
Midnight's march is here.

Dragging tails and growling softly,
Creatures pace the street,
Prowling through the neighbourhood
On giant padded feet.

In the east, the sun is rising,
Creatures creep away.
Hiding where they've always hidden,
Frightened of the day.

Flying Home

I was a long way from home. The light in my attic window was a golden point, far across the valley. I stood in the top of a tree so old that its dappled branches were as wide as pathways. The night was still and warm and a full moon hung in the sky.

I could see the silver river winding down to the coast, smooth paddocks, dark gullies and the distant hills. Far out to the east, I saw the ocean, glinting and moving.

A mopoke called from the bush.
Om…Om…Om…

I leant out of the tree and flew into the still night air. Flying was effortless.

I simply held my arms out like wings and soared, without fear, just above the treetops. The cows and horses looked up as my shadow crossed over them and I called down. 'Hello horses, hello cows.'

A blanket of fine mist hovered over the river and I swooped below it, almost touching the surface. Deep in the clear dark water, spotted trout slept between ribbons of weed.

I followed the river towards the sea as it wound through the marshes, between pale sand dunes and over the beach, scattering terns as

I went. I swept around the bay, flying just above the waves as they rolled to shore, glassy and fat in the moonlight. Shiny dolphins shot through the swells, rolling and twisting, as liquid as the ocean itself.

When I reached our cove I turned towards the hill, slowing as I floated over the paddocks and the orchard. I landed as softly as an owl in the big tree outside our house.

Mr Cat was asleep on my bed, and when I tapped on the glass he came over and opened the window.

'Hello,' he said. 'It's a change for me to be letting you in.'

I climbed into bed and he curled into the bend behind my knees, purring with happiness.

The Long Shadow

Only a little while back,
while working at my desk,
I looked out of the window
and saw a man moving very slowly
past my front gate.

Backwards!

A scorching 43-degree sun
was behind him and at the end
of a blue lead
was a very small and very old dog.

I came to the front gate,
and as the man continued carefully
on his way he told me this:
his dog had very poor eyes,
his dog had cataracts.

They both shuffled on,
the dog's face protected from the sun
by the man's shadow.
I came inside and made this picture.

My Shadow

I have a shadow that follows me everywhere.
When I get up in the morning
my shadow's there to greet me.

My shadow can run.
My shadow can jump.
When I dive into the billabong for a swim,
my shadow always follows.
We have fun.

KAREN BRIGGS & PAUL SEDEN

Sometimes,

once we're finished

with running

and jumping

and swimming,

we'll just sit and have a scratch.

We'll do nothing.

And that's fun, too.

I love my shadow.

'Come on,

let's go have a kick.'

KAREN BRIGGS & PAUL SEDEN

Doctor Maddie

HoneyBear wasn't feeling too good.

Her eyes were droopy.

Her mouth was sad.

Her fur was sticky where someone had spilled Milo on her.

Doctor Maddie said, 'Don't worry, HoneyBear, I'll fix you up, because I'm the best doctor in all the hoss-ti-pal.' She meant to say 'hospital' but it was a hard word to say because she wasn't a real doctor and she was only six years old.

Doctor Maddie cancelled her appointment with Green Giraffe and rescheduled her 10 a.m. with Tartan Tiger. Then she went and got her little brother, Doctor Louie, who was in the living room doing colouring-in.

She also got Nurse Dad, who was in the kitchen playing a game on his phone. (Nurse Dad played a lot of Lolly Level. He really needed to go on a Lolly Level diet.)

They all stood around HoneyBear's bed, then Doctor Maddie said, 'Okay, HoneyBear, just relax, it won't hurt, and you'll soon feel ALLLLLLLL better.'

She turned on her special amazing Special-Amazing Fixing-Machine and she started fixing HoneyBear.

DANNY KATZ & MITCH VANE

Doctor Louie made machine-noises like, 'BEEP BIP BIP.' And Nurse Dad won 800 points on Lolly Level.

Pretty soon HoneyBear started feeling better. Her face looked happier. Her fur even looked less sticky.

'Well done, everyone!' said Doctor Maddie to her team.

'Thanks,' said Doctor Louie, who went back to the living room to finish his colouring-in.

'No probs,' said Nurse Dad, who went back to the kitchen to finish his Lolly Level game.

Doctor Maddie went back to her office. She had lots to do. Mr Booshy, the dinosaur, had been waiting twenty minutes for his check-up. He had a broken bendy tail, and he wasn't too happy at all. Doctor Maddie said, 'Don't worry, Mr Booshy, I'll fix you up, because I'm the best doctor in all the hoss-ti-pal.'

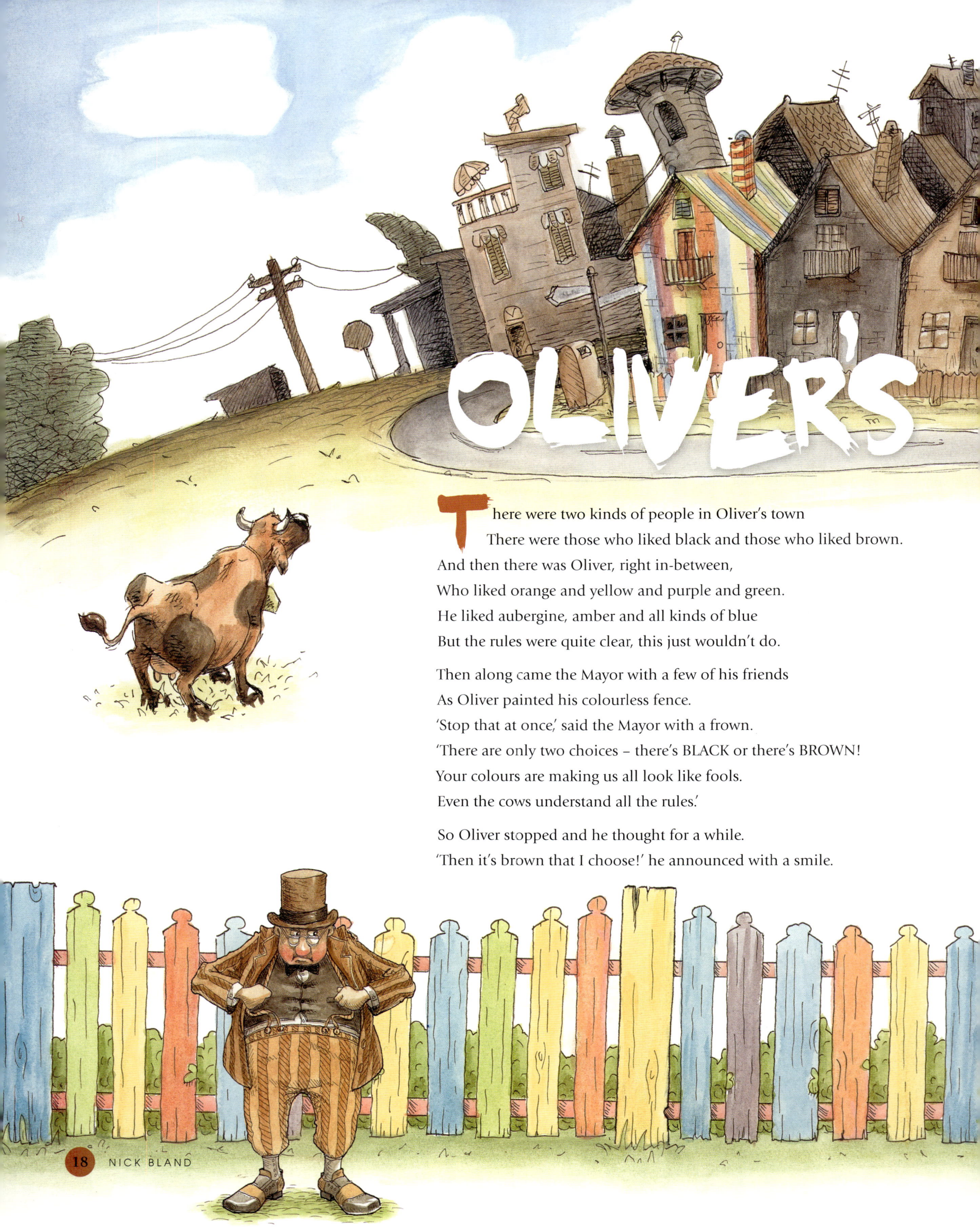

OLIVER'S

There were two kinds of people in Oliver's town
There were those who liked black and those who liked brown.
And then there was Oliver, right in-between,
Who liked orange and yellow and purple and green.
He liked aubergine, amber and all kinds of blue
But the rules were quite clear, this just wouldn't do.

Then along came the Mayor with a few of his friends
As Oliver painted his colourless fence.
'Stop that at once,' said the Mayor with a frown.
'There are only two choices – there's BLACK or there's BROWN!
Your colours are making us all look like fools.
Even the cows understand all the rules.'

So Oliver stopped and he thought for a while.
'Then it's brown that I choose!' he announced with a smile.

TOWN

He mixed up some yellow, some blue and some red.
'I can even add purple and orange!' he said.
'If I stir in some aqua… and turquoise… and green,
It's the finest of browns that has ever been seen.
So you see there's no problem that needs to be fixed.
I love using brown… but my brown is UN-MIXED.'

'My goodness, you're right!' said the brown-wearing Mayor
Then he took off his hat and revealed… ORANGE HAIR.
'So my hair,' said the Mayor, 'from what I have seen…
Is really just brown without purple and green.
I don't even LIKE wearing hats,' he exclaimed.
'I hereby declare that the rule shall be changed.'

Now some prefer black and others like brown
But everyone's welcome in Oliver's town.

GHOST

'Thorry,' said the bloke at the reception desk. He didn't look sorry. He looked grumpy. The peg on his nose didn't help make him look friendly either. 'The resort is closed till dey get the sewage pumped out and the pipe mended.'

Dad glanced at the dark outside. 'But we've driven all day! There must be somewhere we can stay, just for the night.'

The man shrugged. 'Do you want to wade ankle-deep through—'

'No,' said Mum quickly. 'I want the Rosewater Spa in the brochure! I want hot stone massages. I want to relax!'

'I want the circus-skills workshop!' said Deirdre, briefly stopping her cartwheels across the reception area.

I just want everyone to be happy, thought Dougie.

'Thorry,' said the man. 'Can't help you. We're the only resort in the area and…'

A small brown lumpy wave crept towards them across the reception carpet.

The man raced for the door. 'We're closed. Now!'

""

It was going to be a perfect weekend,' mourned Mum as they crammed back into the car, not quite leaving the stink of sewage behind them.

Dad shrugged as Mum started the engine. 'You know what I'd like? An old-fashioned motel, like the ones when I was a kid. Those big breakfasts on a tray they slid into the special window thingy beside the door. Fishing all day and fish and chips at night…'

He shrugged again. 'If we take turns driving we can be home by morning. You kids can nap in the back.'

Huh, thought Dougie, as Deirdre

practised her 'how to tie a knot with your legs behind your neck' manoeuvre next to him.

The car flowed through the night. The road was deserted. Deirdre stopped her gymnastics exercises. But no one slept. Dougie could feel disappointment as thick as the resort's brown sludge seeping through the car.

They'd looked forward to this weekend so much…

All we wanted was a holiday, he thought, *a holiday for all of us*. He shut his eyes. *Please*, he thought, *let there be a resort open that we missed on the way here. Please*…

He opened his eyes.

Nothing. Black trees. Black night. Black road. A faint haze of red and blue.

He blinked. The haze grew brighter. It was a sign, right on the highway – *Rosemary Motel*.

'Look!' he yelled.

'At what?' asked Dad tiredly.

'Go to sleep,' said Mum, staring grimly at the road.

'Look, over there!'

'There's nothing—' began Dad, then stopped.

Vacancies, read the sign. Behind it was a carpark and a line of motel units.

'The Rosemary Motel and Spa!' cried Mum.

'Circus workshop every morning,' said Deirdre. She wriggled her toes above her head in excitement.

'Vacancies!' yelled Dad.

'But…' said Dougie. There was nothing about a spa on the sign. Or circus workshops. But Mum was already parking next to the office.

Dougie followed his family inside.

'Three interconnecting rooms with ensuite bathrooms. Of course.' The woman at the desk looked hungry, as if she hadn't had her dinner yet. She wore a flowered dress and bright green glasses that turned up at the edges and…

Dougie blinked again. The woman at the desk wore jeans and a T-shirt. There was something in her smile.

Like a crocodile that hasn't eaten for a fortnight, thought Dougie. *Like there's no way a big bowl of pasta would fill her up*.

MICHAEL CAMILLERI & JACKIE FRENCH

The receptionist handed them each a key. 'Down on the left,' she said. 'You can't miss them.'

'Breakfast…' began Dad.

'The circus-skills class,' said Deirdre, who was now upside down.

'Everything you need is in the brochure in your room.' The woman smiled again. It seemed to light up the darkness outside. For a moment Dougie's unease ebbed.

'Sleep well,' said the receptionist brightly.

'We will,' said Mum fervently.

I won't, thought Dougie. He looked to the road beyond the carpark, then stopped. Because there was no road. No sign, either. Dougie blinked. It was just the darkness, he told himself. They'd turned the vacancy sign off now they had guests.

He opened his eyes. Starlight shone down on the small squat motel and the gravel carpark with just their car in it, looking strangely faint.

'Mum—' he began.

'Not now,' said Mum with a yawn.

'Something's not right—'

'Dougie, whatever it is, it can wait till the morning when we've had a decent sleep,' said Dad. 'Look, your room's here.'

Dougie opened the door and saw a narrow bed with a pink ruffly bedspread. A shiny-topped table… Then he blinked. On second look, Dougie saw a king-sized bed with buffalo horns above it. A giant TV screen. A wall full of books.

Books? He'd never seen books in a resort before.

'Dad—' he tried again.

'Tomorrow,' said Dad firmly.

Dougie heard the other doors slam shut.

Dougie couldn't sleep. There was no way he could sleep in a place like this …

Dougie opened his eyes as something clattered near the door. It was morning. He looked at the clock on the bedside table. Ten o'clock! He'd never slept that late before.

There was a knock on the door and Dad bounced in. A happy dad, all rested and relaxed, in the horrible green socks Deirdre had given him for Christmas.

'Breakfast!' Dad announced. He gestured to a small cupboard in the wall by the door. Dougie hadn't noticed it last night.

'I filled in the breakfast form for you and me last night. Your mum and Deirdre are having the buffet breakfast. Then your mum's booked in all day at the spa and Deirdre has her circus-skills workshop.' Dad pulled the tray out of the cupboard and set it out on the table by the window.

Dougie pulled open the curtains. A patio with potted flowers looked out over a gleaming white sand beach. Dougie remembered he'd seen a river marked on the resort's map.

'Great, isn't it?' grinned Dad. 'How about you and me go fishing? There are fishing lines for hire and they'll cook anything we catch—'

'But, Dad—'

'This is going to be the best holiday ever,' said Dad.

Dougie crossed the room and peered out the other window. Their car still sat there, alone. At least he could see the highway now, though there weren't any cars on it. Maybe he'd just missed it in the dark last night.

Dougie checked out the breakfast Dad had ordered. Bowls of fresh fruit salad – cherries, chopped watermelon, sliced apples, oranges and peaches. Two plates of scrambled eggs. Baked tomato. Tiny gleaming sausages. Baked beans. Small mounds of spinach. The thickest toast he'd ever seen, in a silver rack. Little bowls of butter, strawberry jam, apricot jam. A pot of honey. A coffee pot. Two glasses of orange juice so fresh they had little blobs of fruit on the rim.

'Just like when I was a boy!' said Dad. 'I've always wanted to share some of those days with you. Fishing in the river. Listening to the birds and the water. Then talking – just you and me, Dougie-boy. Now eat up. We're going to have a perfect day.'

'But…' Dougie began.

Then something flowed through him. A wistfulness. A longing. For Dad to be happy. For Mum to be relaxed. For Deirdre to hang upside down so long that next week she wouldn't mind being crammed into a school desk most of the day. And other longings, too. Strange ones he didn't have words for.

Dougie couldn't spoil his family's day. He picked up his orange juice.

It *was* a perfect day. The motel had a 'tinnie' – a boat that was a bit like a big tin can – that Dad rowed into the middle of the river. He and Dougie sat there in hats and sunblock and ate tomato sandwiches and vegemite and lettuce rolls ('Just like when I was a kid,' said Dad again) and frozen cordial that slowly unfroze and dribbled down your throat as you tipped up the bottle. The lines dangled in the water and drifted with the current. And they talked, after a million birds had talked to them first. They talked about Grandpa and a war called Vietnam, something Dougie had never heard Dad talk about before. And as the shadows stretched across the river Dougie talked too, about what it felt like when maths went RIGHT instead of wrong and how the girl with the red plaits on his school bus had smiled at him last week…

And then their lines jerked. 'Reel it in. Slowly now,' whispered Dad. And Dougie did, as Dad reeled his as well, to discover two big silver fish that were the most alive things he had ever seen, but somehow dinner too.

It was late when they returned to the motel. Mum and Deirdre had already eaten.

'It was the best day,' said Mum, smiling and relaxed as she lay on the bed, the movie on pause. 'That hot stone massage!'

'I want a trapeze for Christmas,' said Deirdre as she balanced on one hand on a chair on the table. 'They have a dinner buffet, but with pizza too if you want it, and an ice-cream bar…'

Dougie and Dad ordered from room service. They ate fish and chips, the  chips fatter and crisper than any Dougie had ever eaten, while they watched *The Princess Bride*, which had been Dad's favourite movie when he was a kid and just happened to be on TV in Dougie's room when they switched it on. And Dad was right. Somehow you could love fish and catch it and even eat it – as long as someone else did the messy bits. It was the best he'd ever eaten, like tasting the river and the sun…

And then they went to bed.

☗

Dougie lay in his bed with the buffalo horns. It had been the most perfect day of his life. And Dad's and Mum's and Deirdre's. And it wasn't right because there were still no cars on the highway out the front. And where was the spa that Mum had been to? And the circus tent for Deirdre's trapeze? There wasn't even room for the buffet in the tiny reception.

But mostly it was a feeling. A feeling that there should be other guests here, on a long weekend when the nearest other resort was shut. A feeling…

What was the feeling?

And suddenly he had it – a hungry feeling, like the rooms, the motel itself had been waiting and was now gobbling them up. Dougie's body froze. He forced himself out of bed, over to the window. He pushed aside the curtains.

Their car was still there, alone in the carpark. On Monday morning they could drive away. Or could they?

Dougie sat back on the bed, his heart thumping. Should he run to Mum and Dad now, get them up, urge them to jump in the car and drive and drive, away from this impossible motel and their impossibly happy weekend…

He stopped. For they *were* happy. He had never seen Dad as happy, like all the happiness Dad had known as a kid was back for Dougie to share now. Had never seen Mum as relaxed, all the stress of work steam-massaged out of her. Never seen Deirdre so excited about flying through the air.

One more day, he thought. *We're only staying here one more day.* Surely it would make no difference if they left now, or tried to leave on Monday morning. One more day and one more night.

What could happen in one more day? A happy day…

☗

It was a happy day.

Dougie and Dad fished from the riverbank, sitting on the sandy verge and, when the fish didn't bite, suddenly they were building a sandcastle. Dougie was too old to build sandcastles but not this one – a circle of grand turrets with a moat. They ate more sandwiches and cut into a vast watermelon Dad had rolled down to the sand, and just as they started eating the first hunks Mum arrived, all glowing from her massage, then Deirdre too, walking on her hands.

And suddenly the four of them had watermelon juice dripping down their chins and sandy sticky hands and the castle got bigger and more grand. Behind them the motel's blank windows watched. And Dougie thought, *It isn't hungry now. Just for a little while, it isn't hungry.*

Nor were they.

As the darkness settled across the river they finished the castle and ambled back to the lights of the motel. They sat around the table in Mum and Dad's room and shared a giant pizza and more watermelon. Then they played Scrabble from the game that had appeared in the breakfast cupboard.

The next morning it was time to drive home. Dougie held his breath as they put their room keys back on the counter. The woman wore another flowered dress, blue and white this time, and her glasses were bright purple, but when Dougie blinked it was jeans again, and no glasses at all.

'I hope you enjoyed your stay?' she said. Dougie let his breath out and took another, so he'd have enough breath to shout or run, because he could see the hunger in the woman's gaze as she asked the question. He could feel… something… in the air.

We are their only guests. Can they really let us go? he thought.

'We had the best weekend ever,' said Dad.

'The best,' said Mum and Deirdre together.

'The very best,' said Dougie, staring at the woman, daring her to do anything to his family to take the joy away.

'I'm glad,' she said. Dougie wondered if she winked at him as they left.

The car started. He'd thought it mightn't, but it did. The highway was there, too, as they drove out and down the road. Mum and Deirdre talked about putting up a tightrope in the garage when they got home. Dougie peered back towards the motel. He knew before he looked what he would see.

Nothing. Not a sign or even a carpark. Just trees and the long road behind.

He looked at his family. Should he say, 'Look back! There's nothing there!'? Then they'd know that their happiness had been an illusion and… No, it hadn't been, he realised. He had been happy. They were still happy. The motel might have been an illusion, but the happiness was not.

'Petrol,' said Dad, turning into a garage.

Dad filled the tank while Dougie bought some chewing gum. He handed the money to the old man at the till.

'Got a touch of sun,' said the old man.

'Yes,' said Dougie. He hesitated. 'When I was fishing. We've been staying at the motel down the road.'

'The Rosemary?'

Dougie nodded.

'Ah,' said the old man. He looked at Dougie. Dougie looked back.

'Burnt down in the bushfire in 1969,' said the old man expressionlessly. 'I was about your age then.'

Dougie said nothing.

'You had a good time?'

'Yes,' said Dougie.

'Ah,' said the old man again. He glanced out at Dougie's family settling back into the car, then at another customer looking at the packaged pies. He bent his head and said quietly, 'I took my family there once. Best weekend we ever had. Couldn't take them a second time, of course.'

No, thought Dougie. Because the second time they might just notice the motel they thought they'd seen, the exact motel they'd longed for, wasn't really there.

'Always was a good place to have a happy time,' said the old man. 'Always will be, I reckon.'

'Dougie!' called Mum.

Dougie nodded at the man. He picked up his gum and walked back to the car. But he was smiling now. What would the ghost of a motel want, after so many years of making people happy? Just to do it again… and again and again.

And somewhere, carried on the breeze, Dougie heard the sound of children's laughter.

I'm not afraid of the waiting room,
the way it always smells like waiting
as the world goes on outside without me.
I'm not afraid of doctors and nurses
their friendly soft footfalls down long corridors
quiet as unspoken facts in folders.

I'm not afraid of antiseptic rooms, of theatres.
I like the brightness. I like the benevolent round edges. The metal and linen.
They are ready to take me in now.

The strange machines, I know them all.
Kind voices have explained everything, the tubes and lights and drips and clicks.
There is nothing to worry about. I know, I know. This I know. But still.

The owl is waiting.

White on white, soft feathers can't hide the black needle tips.
I listen to what they are always telling me and try not to look,
even as I stretch out my naked arm.

Accept it, I tell myself, accept the weight of big claws stepping up.
Breathe, keep breathing, as they grasp my skin.
Now higher, high on my shoulder. Resist the urge to run.

Breathe, keep breathing, as it settles on my chest,
talons on my collarbone, and they say, 'You may feel a pressure.'
And so it comes.

Wings expand around my ears, filling the room.

I promise myself I will not cry, I promise
even as the arctic heat thrums against my tight-shut eyes,
even when it feels like I'm drowning in feathers.

Think that friends and family will be here soon
letting me know how brave I am. How strong.
Think of warm hands and safe words, flowers and cards, hopes and wishes.

And later, try not to look to the other side of the bed,
how it stays behind when all visitors have left,
softly breathing in and out, with nothing to say.

Ignore the click of talons on the railing,
the big lighthouse eyes that turn to stare and turn away again,
as if casting over an invisible void.

It will never know my name. It will never know how I feel.
It only knows one thing, this one cold fact always guarded in silence:
In time you will be well again.

Until then the owl will never leave my side.
It will caress me the only way it can, with claws and feathers,
and every time I reach out to it in fear, I reach out in gladness.

Because owls are never wrong.

I am the small green pea
you are the tender pod
hold me

I am the diving kite
you are the bow-tied tail
steady me

I am the drifting boat
you are the quiet deep
buoy me

I am the stumbling words
you are the melody
sing me

I am the crimsoned leaf
you are the whispered breeze
dance with me

I am the sapphire night
you are the milken moon
light me

I am the thirsting earth
you are the jewelled rain
fill me

I am the falling star
you are the wishful hands
catch me

I am the padlocked door
you are the loving key
open me

I
you
we

Biscuit and Bones

On summer days Bones liked to roll on his back and watch clouds float by. Biscuit barked at butterflies.

Bones always rose to greet loved ones with a loyal wag of his tail. Biscuit gave slobbery licks and puppy kisses in exchange for a belly scratch.

Although Bones couldn't dig as deep as he used to, he still believed in miracles. So Biscuit dug holes, all over the garden, and they gnawed on buried treasure.

MARK GREENWOOD & FRANÉ LESSAC

Bones was never afraid to leave the yard and make friends with dogs who looked different. He taught Biscuit to smell the roses – not pee on them.

Biscuit and Bones never passed up a ride to the beach, wind in their faces, the wonder of soft sand, chasing things that made them happy.

Some days even Biscuit needed a quiet moment.
He would roll on his back in the soft grass and snuggle up to his friend.
Together they'd watch the clouds float by
and wonder, where did yesterday go?

DOT THE TOT

Dot was not
the kind of tot
to sit around
and stay.

'Sit quietly, now,'
were not the words
that gladdened
poor Dot's day.

Dot liked words like

SHOUT and **run** and **jump** and **bounce** and **sing!**

'Sit quietly, Dot,'
her mum would say.
'And don't do anything.'

So Dot would sit
and it was tough.
The clock would tick
and soon enough…

Dot's limbs would twitch,
her nose would itch,
her fingers pick,
her small feet kick.

She'd start to wriggle,
her foot would jiggle,
until deep down
she'd feel a giggle.

Above her chin
her mouth would grin,
her knees would knock
her head would rock,
her ears would flap,
one hand would tap,
as she'd wait for
her mum to

SNAP!

Dot was NOT
the kind of tot
to sit around and stay

Until one day
Dot's mum said, 'Hey!
I've got a game to play.'

So now Dot sits
and really it's
AMAZING but it's true.

Dot the tot
has learned to play
a game she calls

statue.

The Best Horse of All

One hot and dusty day the carousel came to town. Everyone queued quickly to buy tickets. Emily was last. She was always last. By the time Emily had bought her ticket there was only one horse left. But it wasn't a proper horse. It was a seahorse!

The other children patted the manes of their horses. They jiggled the reins. They called, 'Giddy up!' And they felt sorry for Emily with her arms around the neck of the pot-bellied little seahorse.

'Don't be disappointed,' whispered the carousel man. 'This is the best horse of all.'

'Really?' said Emily.

'Hold tight,' said the man.

Slowly, the carousel started to go round, and the music began. Swirling, exciting rhythms and sounds made Emily think of galloping wild horses. Her heart thumped. The carousel was speeding up, too, going faster and faster, until everything began to blur and spin…

As if from a long way away, Emily heard the seahorse call, 'Take a deep breath! Here we go!'

Before Emily could ask, 'Where to?' they were plunging into the warm, tropical waters of a coral reef that blazed with colour – rich reds, blues, yellows, greens.

Swimming alongside clownfish and angelfish, Emily patted a sea cow and touched the fin of a manta ray.

Finally, the seahorse swam slowly through a seagrass meadow. It swayed, its tail twirled around a strand of grass.

'Time to go back,' it said.

'Not yet!' cried Emily. 'Please.'

But the seahorse said, 'I'm sorry, but the music is calling us.'

Once more everything began to blur and spin…

Emily looked around, her eyes wide. She touched her hair with wonder. It was wet!

The carousel had stopped, and children were hopping off their horses.

But Emily stayed for a while, stroking the pot-bellied little seahorse, the best horse of all.

JULIE VIVAS & MARGARET WILD

Recipe to Catch a Wish

Ingredients

1. A touch of magic – can be found in the hugs of someone with very curly or very straight hair. Someone without hair will also do.
2. One small teacup. If actual teacup is unavailable then an imaginary one will do.
3. A single tear from a happy moment – yours or someone else's.
4. Your favourite stuffed toy.

Method

1. Place the single tear in the teacup.
2. Think about the hug and blow over the teacup.
3. Shake hands with your favourite stuffed toy and politely ask if you may borrow some fluff.
4. Place fluff in the teacup.
5. Scrunch up your toes as tight as can be and whisper the most ridiculous word you can think of.

Your wish should now be floating gently above you, ready for use. Beware, however, that while all wishes do come true, it is often in unexpected ways!

POPPY

Once upon a night-time, just after the midnight hour, Poppy woke up in her brand-new prawn onesie. She looked into the mirror, and sighed.

If I ruled the whole world, the birds would always sing the sun would always shine the flowers would never die.

Gggggggrrrrrrr growled Wolfie the dog.

Yes, Wolfie, and you would have all the treats you can eat, Poppy said.

Outside the wind began to howl. Poppy's head turned upside down. She was looking straight at the spidery stars. Oh no! she said, What good is an upside-down head? My baked beans my sardines my ice-creams will all
f
a
l
l out.

ooooooOOOOOoooooOOOOOOOOOOOoo

Wolfie was scared.

CHRIS MCKIMMIE

HUSH, WOLFIE!

Poppy hissed, but her words came out all wrong, like this:
Flush Who ie?
Wolfie went growly mad.
Ti pots!
Poppy shouted.
QUIET!
Poppy's words and world began to slip slowly back into place. The early birds were singing. The sun began to shine.

See, Wolfie, I am still me, she said.

G GGG GRrrr rrrr rr rrr r

Grandma's Treasure

Amelia woke with butterflies flitting and fluttering through her as she stretched out her arms and legs. Today she was going to Grandma's house for an overnight stay and she couldn't wait to ring Grandma to remind her.

'Oh, how wonderful, darling, I'll get to see my treasure,' said Grandma.

Treasure?

Amelia had stayed overnight at Grandma's many times before but she had never seen any treasure. Thoughts danced through her mind as she wondered where it could be.

Amelia adored Grandma's house.

She loved… the heavy pink petals sprinkled like giant confetti on the driveway, and the warm sweetness of baking cakes.

Most of all, she loved Grandma – her soft, powdery smell and the twinkle in her eye.

Grandma's house felt like the safest place on earth.

Grandma was waiting with a big warm hug when Amelia arrived later that morning. She took Amelia's things inside and laid them at the end of the bed next to hers. This was Amelia's very own special bed. The bedspreads were deep blue velvet, all heavy and smooth. Amelia quickly peeked under the bed, but there was no treasure there.

'Cake time!' called Grandma from the kitchen. At Grandma's house there were no rules at breakfast. Amelia ran down the long hallway that led to the kitchen and tucked straight into a piece of Grandma's amazing chocolate mud cake. The icing oozed deliciously, and Amelia licked it off each and every finger.

'Look, Grandma,' said Amelia. 'It looks like mud! Is this why it's called "mud cake"?'

Grandma laughed her musical laugh. 'I think it might just be,' she said. 'Now wash up. It's a lovely sunny day outside, let's do some gardening.'

Grandma's garden was like a big park, with leafy trees and flowers of every colour. *A perfect place for hiding treasure*, Amelia thought. She searched the garden and something caught her eye behind the garden shed; a bright red glow beneath the green patches of leaves on the ground.

'Rubies!' whispered Amelia. She folded back the leaves to find…

Grandma's ripe, juicy strawberries!

'Amelia,' said Grandma, 'you've found my beauties! Let's pick these for later. Then you can help me find something I put under the house for safekeeping.'

Ooh… the treasure! thought Amelia.

As Grandma unlocked the little wooden door that led under the house, Amelia skipped in circles. It was dark and a little bit scary in there. Amelia stayed close to Grandma and tried not to be frightened by the spiders' webs that hung near their heads. Grandma searched through box after box, and each time Amelia was sure that the treasure must be in the next one.

'How about this one?' Amelia asked, pointing to a small tin box.

'Wonderful girl,' Grandma cried. 'You've found my button box! Now I can finish sewing the dress I've been making for you.'

A new dress! Amelia thought excitedly. But with no treasure under the house, she would have to keep looking.

While Grandma was sewing Amelia's dress, Amelia checked the dolls' cupboard on the verandah, but there was no treasure there. She checked the bookshelf near the cupboard as well, carefully shaking each book upside down in case the treasure fell out. Then she remembered another special cupboard that was in a bedroom behind a closed door.

VICTORIA ROHAN & JANE TANNER

I bet that's where the treasure is hidden, she thought.

Tiptoeing down the hallway, Amelia held her breath. She crept past the sewing room and the busy whirr of Grandma's sewing machine. She snuck through the kitchen, quietly opening each cupboard door, but there was nothing unusual there. She went into the dining room, stopping to look at the paintings on the walls. Finally, she took a deep breath and pushed the bedroom door open.

Amelia looked carefully under the pink velvet bedspread that was like the blue bedspreads in Grandma's bedroom. She opened each of the drawers in the big desk that sat against the wall and looked behind the armchair that sat against the window.

Finally, when she had checked every corner of the room, Amelia turned to the huge dark wooden cupboard with the key in it. She stretched up as high as she could to turn the key, and the door opened with a whack! A shiny perfect doll with blinking eyes fell onto the floor.

Amelia got such a fright! She picked the doll up, sat it on the desk, and decided that was enough hunting for one day.

That night, as Grandma tucked her under the blue velvet bedspread, the butterflies in Amelia's stomach started fluttering in opposite directions. She felt awful for going into the bedroom with the closed door.

'Grandma?' she whispered in a tiny voice. Her tears began to flow. 'I've been looking for your treasure all day.'

'What do you mean, darling?' Grandma sounded puzzled.

'You said you would see your treasure today,' Amelia sniffled. 'I thought I saw rubies in the garden, but it was just the strawberry patch. And… and then I thought you'd hidden the treasure under the house with the horrible scary spiders… and, and the room, sorry, I went into the room with the closed door—'

'What are you talking about, Amelia?' interrupted Grandma.

'Your treasure, Grandma,' blurted out Amelia. 'I've… I've been trying to find your… treasure.'

Grandma smiled tenderly as she put her arms around Amelia and wiped a tear from her cheek. 'Oh, my darling,' she said. 'Don't you know? You're my treasure!'

And as Amelia drifted off to sleep under the deep blue covers, she had never felt more special.

contributors

KEVIN BURGEMEESTRE
The cover sculpture reflects my love of story and adventure. I'm a writer and illustrator who thinks children are the very best audience.

MICHAEL CAMILLERI
I drew the spooky motel. I illustrate and make comics and theatre. I like a beautiful idea and a good scare!

JACKIE FRENCH
I wanted to write a story about being happy. That's what was so inspiring about these kids, their families and the Hush project: finding happiness.

JANE GODWIN
I am a publisher and author. Anna Walker and I have created several picture books together, and we have lots of fun collaborating.

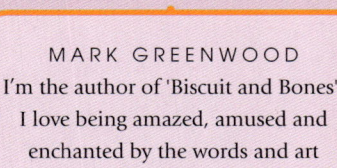

MARK GREENWOOD
I'm the author of 'Biscuit and Bones'. I love being amazed, amused and enchanted by the words and art of picture books.

BOB GRAHAM
Dogs have always been part of my life. They still lie on my bed, push me off the couch, and make themselves quite at home in my stories.

KAREN BRIGGS
I illustrated 'My Shadow' in this book. I love to inspire children through my artwork and give them some imagination to support the storyline.

NICK BLAND
The Royal Children's Hospital staff saved my life when I was a baby, so the least I could do was write and illustrate a story for this book.

JACQUI GRANTFORD
I love the magic that can light up a child's face, and I'm thrilled to be part of this book, which will create that magic.

LEE BURGEMEESTRE
I designed this book. I'm a graphic designer and illustrator and I've always loved the heart and humour of children's books.

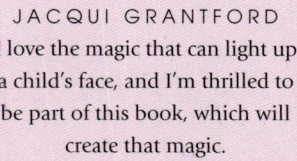

ALISON LESTER
When I was a little girl I dreamt I could fly. Gliding home above the trees was a magical feeling, and I hope I've passed that on.

GLENDA MILLARD
One day when I was sad my friend Stephen sent me some music. I listened, then wrote this poem. Proof that friends plus music equals happiness.

CHRIS MCKIMMIE
I am an illustrator, author and designer. Picture books are like haikus to me. You can say a lot with very little.

ANN JAMES
I illustrated 'Dot the Tot' – and helped Kevin and Lee create the crowd of characters from these Hush stories that come to life on the endpapers!

TOHBY RIDDLE
I write and illustrate picture books and draw cartoons. I like using words and pictures to show ideas – because ideas can take you anywhere.

STEPHEN MICHAEL KING
My studio is on a windswept hill, atop a coastal island. I'm at my happiest when I catch a great idea floating by.

JUDITH ROSSELL
I drew the maze page. I am an illustrator and writer, and I love designing puzzles for people to solve.

DANNY KATZ
I wrote a story in this book called 'Doctor Maddie'. If you don't like it, Mitch Vane wrote it.

DOUG MACLEOD
I'm a TV writer; I rarely write verse now. As a kid, most of my favourite tales were in verse. It was fun and nostalgic to write this rhyme.

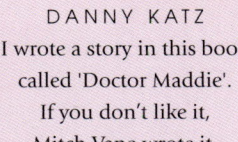

FRANÉ LESSAC
I'm the illustrator of 'Biscuit and Bones'. I spend a lot of time flying through clouds and dreaming up paintings to share.

BRUCE WHATLEY
I'm an author/illustrator who refuses to grow up. A big kid up to my knees in children's books!

SHAUN TAN
'Ward' was inspired by a visit to The Royal Children's Hospital, and meeting a little girl there who was bravely undergoing treatment.

KAREN TAYLEUR
Here's to all the Dots in the world who cannot possibly stop, no matter what!

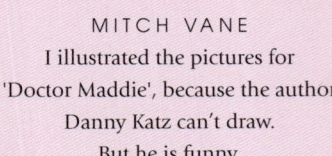

MITCH VANE
I illustrated the pictures for 'Doctor Maddie', because the author Danny Katz can't draw. But he is funny.

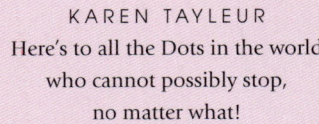

ANNA WALKER
I am an illustrator and storyteller. I love escaping to a place where armadillos roam and goldfish swim in trees.

MARGARET WILD
I've been writing children's books since 1984 and it still gives me such pleasure and joy.

PAUL SEDEN
I adore the creativity of picture books and the like-minded families that read them; I've enjoyed being a small part of this one for you.

JANE TANNER
I draw to understand what is real. In 'Grandma's Treasure' the love between Grandma and her treasured Amelia felt very real.

VICTORIA ROHAN
My love of children's literature commenced with my Grandma. This story is for all those 'treasures' out there.

CRAIG SMITH
Thanks to *all* the Hush team for including me in this project. It brightened my day – so I tried to paint that.

JULIE VIVAS
I illustrated Emily riding the seahorse into the ocean. That is where I'd like to be: under the water, swimming, and watching the fish.

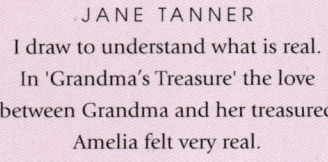